ABE LINCOLN
HIS WIT AND WISDOM
FROM A–Z

BY **ALAN SCHROEDER**

ILLUSTRATED BY
JOHN O'BRIEN

Holiday House / New York

A is for *Amendment*

After Abraham Lincoln became president in 1861, he worked hard to put an end to slavery. In 1863 he signed the Emancipation Proclamation, which freed some slaves. Then, in 1865, he pushed for passage of the Thirteenth Amendment to the Constitution, which would outlaw slavery forever in the United States.

For Lincoln it was a tough battle, but on January 31, 1865, the Thirteenth Amendment was passed by Congress. In the House of Representatives, men sent up cheers, women fluttered handkerchiefs, and African Americans wept tears of joy. The Emancipation Proclamation is better known, but the Thirteenth Amendment was in some ways Lincoln's most important and far-reaching accomplishment.

THIRTEENTH AMENDMENT

If slavery is not wrong, nothing is wrong.

Aloud – Lincoln had a lifelong habit of reading aloud. Speaking aloud an idea, he said, helped him to better remember it.

I don't know who my grandfather was; I am much more concerned to know what his grandson will be.

Autobiography – In 1859, when Lincoln was getting ready to run for president, he wrote a campaign autobiography. It was only 600 words long. "There is not much of it," he told a friend, "for the reason, I suppose, that there is not much of me." Abe Lincoln was a modest man.

Ax – Abe Lincoln was raised in the backwoods of Indiana. When he was seven, his father handed him an ax and told him to start clearing land. Abe said that for the next sixteen years he almost always had an ax in his hand.

Leave nothing for to-morrow which can be done to-day.

B is for *Black Hawk War*

In 1832, when he was twenty-three, Abraham Lincoln participated in the Black Hawk War, in which Illinois settlers battled Native Americans who were defending their lands. Lincoln served three months, first as a captain, then as a private. It was the only military experience of his career. Like many young soldiers, Abe looked forward to seeing some action at the front. But the only bloody battles he fought, he said, were with mosquitoes.

Board – When Abe was young, his family couldn't afford paper, so he wrote on boards. It irritated his father, who did carpentry work, to see perfectly good lumber covered with Abe's scribbling.

We should be too big to take offense and too noble to give it.

Bed – Abe had very long legs. His bed in the White House was nine feet long!

C is for *Civil War*

For four years—from 1861 to 1865—the United States was engulfed in the horror of the Civil War. It distressed Lincoln to see the North and the South tearing each other apart; as president, he spent most of his time searching for ways to bring the conflict to a speedy end.

Cabin – Abraham Lincoln was born in a one-room log cabin in Kentucky on February 12, 1809. A replica of the dirt-floor cabin now stands near the original site and is visited by thousands of people every year.

Commander in Chief – During the Civil War, Lincoln, as president, served as commander in chief of the country's military forces. He took his job as commander seriously, studying maps and reports, meeting frequently with military officers, and helping to devise battlefield strategy.

D is for *Duel*

A man once challenged Abraham Lincoln to a duel, but Lincoln did not want to fight. When offered his choice of weapons, he supposedly answered, "How about cow dung at five paces?"

Draft – During the Civil War the Union army desperately needed soldiers, so Lincoln started the first national draft. Any able-bodied man, he said, who was selected for the draft and tried to get out of it would be sent to jail.

Disapprove – When Mary Todd was dating Abraham Lincoln, her family strongly disapproved of the match. They thought Abe was a country bumpkin, and didn't hesitate to say so.

Dream – While Lincoln was in the White House, he had several dreams about his own death. In one dream he entered a room full of weeping people. He asked a soldier what was wrong. "The president," the soldier answered. "He was killed by an assassin!"

E is for

Emancipation Proclamation

On January 1, 1863, President Lincoln signed the Emancipation Proclamation, which freed most slaves living in the Southern states. It also declared that the U.S. military would begin taking black servicemen into its ranks. Lincoln considered the Emancipation Proclamation his most important act, "the one thing that will make people remember I ever lived."

Edward – Edward Lincoln was the second of Abraham and Mary's four sons. He died in 1850, at the age of three. Mary was so upset by Eddy's death that, for a time, she lost all interest in food. Abe had to beg her to eat.

Equality – Though Lincoln freed the slaves, he did not believe in social equality between blacks and whites. Like "any other man," he said, he was "in favor of having the superior position assigned to the white race." To this day, people are troubled by that statement. It upsets their image of Abraham Lincoln as the "Great Emancipator."

In giving freedom to the slave, we assure freedom to the free.

As I would not be a slave, so I would not be a master. This expresses my idea of democracy.

F is for *Fort Sumter*

The first crisis of Abraham Lincoln's presidency occurred on April 12, 1861, less than six weeks after he had taken office. On that day, Southern rebels fired upon Fort Sumter, a federal arsenal in the harbor of Charleston, South Carolina. For thirty-three hours Confederate artillery battered the fort, until at last the Union commander was forced to surrender. Northerners were outraged by the attack on Fort Sumter and immediately scrambled to raise and equip troops of their own. The Civil War had begun!

Be sure you put your feet in the right place, then stand firm.

UNITED WE STAND.

A house divided against itself cannot stand.

Fable – One of Abe's favorite books as a boy was *Aesop's Fables*. Later, as a lawyer, then congressman, then president, he would remember the fables and try to apply their lessons to his own life. One moral he especially admired: "United we stand, divided we fall."

DIVIDED.

WE FALL.

My concern is not whether God is on our side; my greatest concern is to be on God's side, for God is always right.

G is for *Gettysburg Address*

A great battle was fought at Gettysburg, Pennsylvania, in July of 1863. Four months later, President Lincoln spoke at the dedication of the country's first national cemetery at Gettysburg. Using a few well-chosen words, he paid tribute to the thousands of soldiers who had died there; they had given their lives, he said, "that [our] nation might live." Today the Gettysburg Address is regarded as one of the most powerful and eloquent speeches that Lincoln ever gave.

Globe Tavern – Abraham and Mary Lincoln were married in 1842. Their first home was a room at the Globe Tavern in Springfield, Illinois. It was tiny, but the rent was only four dollars per week.

Good Samaritan – Lincoln wasn't much of a churchgoer, but he was a Good Samaritan, always ready to help someone in need. One bitterly cold night in Indiana, he and a friend found a man lying drunk in the road. Lincoln picked up the man, carried him to a nearby house, lit a fire, and stayed with him all night to make sure that he was all right.

Marriage is neither heaven nor hell, it is simply purgatory.

H is for *Hat*

Lincoln, a tall man, wore a stovepipe hat, which made him look even taller. He used the hat to carry paperwork.

Homestead Act – In 1862 President Lincoln signed the Homestead Act, which gave 160 acres to any man who promised to work the land and live on it for five years. Thousands of people scrambled to take advantage of the government's generous offer.

Honest Abe – When Abe was in his mid-twenties, he and a friend opened a general store in New Salem, Illinois. But neither of them knew what he was doing, and the store failed. Lincoln made sure, though, that all his creditors got paid, and it was then that people began to call him "Honest Abe."

IOWA

KANSAS   MISSOURI

OKLAHOMA

NS.

ILLINOIS

INDIANA

MICHIGAN

LAKE MICHIGAN

LAKE ERIE

NEW YO

KENTUCKY

OHIO

PENNSYLVA

I is for *Indiana* and *Illinois*

Lincoln was born in Kentucky, but when he was seven he moved with his family to Indiana. There, in the woods, Abe's father began chopping down trees to build a log cabin. Indiana in those days was rough country—dangerous, too: Abe had to keep his eyes open for bears, panthers, and other wild animals.

In 1830, when Abe was twenty-one, the Lincoln family moved west to Illinois. There Lincoln married, fathered children, and became a respected lawyer. It was in Illinois, too, that he began his political career. For several years Lincoln served in the Illinois legislature; then he represented the state as a U.S. congressman in Washington, DC. Lincoln lived in Illinois for more than thirty years, until he moved to the White House in 1861.

VIRGINI

Invention – In 1848 Lincoln invented a device to help lift boats that were stuck on sandbars. He had the invention patented, but he never made any money from it. Abraham Lincoln is the only U.S. president to have been awarded a patent.

Invite – Lincoln was the first president to invite a group of free black people to the White House. They arrived on August 14, 1862. It was not, however, a social call. Lincoln wanted to discuss with them the future of the black race in America.

It is better to remain silent and be thought a fool than to open one's mouth and remove all doubt.

MISSISSIPPI

ALABAMA

GEORGIA

SOUTH CAROLINA

is for *Jack*

During the Civil War, Lincoln's two youngest sons, Willie and Tad, enjoyed playing with a soldier doll named Jack. One day they decided that Jack must be shot at sunrise for sleeping while on duty. But then the White House gardener suggested that Jack be pardoned instead. The boys ran to their father, who wrote the official order on White House stationery: "The doll Jack is pardoned. By order of the President. A. Lincoln."

A week later, Willie and Tad discovered that Jack was both a traitor and a spy and sent him to the gallows.

> I have always found that mercy bears richer fruits than strict justice.

Joke – Young Abe once played a joke on his stepmother, Sarah. He had his friends walk barefoot through a mud puddle, then he carried each of them home, lifted them up, and had them "walk" across the ceiling. When Sarah saw the muddy footprints above her head, she burst out laughing. She knew a good joke when she saw one. Sarah and Abe always got along well.

K is for Kentucky

Abe's earliest years were spent in Kentucky. According to a cousin of his, Abe spent his days "fishin' in the crick, settin' traps fur rabbits an' muskrats, goin' on coon-hunts . . . [and] follerin' up bees to find bee-trees. . . . Mighty interestin' life fur a boy."

Kitten – Lincoln loved cats, especially young ones. Few things gave him more pleasure than to spend an hour playing with a kitten.

No matter how much cats fight, there always seem to be plenty of kittens.

Knoll – Lincoln taught himself law by reading law books. His favorite place to study was atop a wooded knoll, where he'd spread out under a tree and read for hours on end.

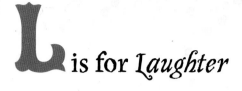is for *Laughter*

Lincoln loved to tell funny stories. During the Civil War, however, some people were offended by his jokes. How could he laugh, they asked, when so many soldiers were suffering? As Lincoln tried to explain, he had to laugh; otherwise he would have no choice but to cry. A friend of his got it right when he said that laughter was "the president's life-preserver!"

Lawyer – Abraham Lincoln worked for many years as a lawyer in Illinois. He had all sorts of clients: husbands and wives who wanted a divorce; people arguing about money or property rights; farmers quarreling over who owned a certain hog or horse. Once, in court, Lincoln defended a rambunctious group of women who caused a riot by breaking up a saloon!

Laughter [is] the joyous, beautiful, universal evergreen of life.

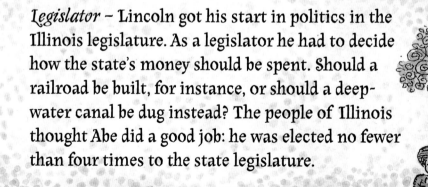

Legislator – Lincoln got his start in politics in the Illinois legislature. As a legislator he had to decide how the state's money should be spent. Should a railroad be built, for instance, or should a deep-water canal be dug instead? The people of Illinois thought Abe did a good job: he was elected no fewer than four times to the state legislature.

The best thing about the future is that it comes one day at a time.

M is for *Mary*

A native of Lexington, Kentucky, Mary Todd became Abraham Lincoln's wife. She was lively and intelligent; she was also ambitious and, at a young age, told friends and family that she intended to marry a future president. Practically from the day she met Abe, she kept him moving forward. She believed in him when no one else did. Without Mary at his side, Abraham Lincoln might never have run for higher office.

After her husband's death in 1865, Mary moved first to Chicago, then to Europe, but she never found peace or happiness. She died in 1882 at the age of sixty-three.

Mexican War – In the late 1840s Lincoln served one term as a congressman in Washington. In the House of Representatives he spoke out vigorously against the Mexican War, insisting that America had no business invading its neighbor. Back home in Illinois, people were shocked when they read Lincoln's speeches. He was called unpatriotic, and after that one term he never served in Congress again.

The man does not live who is more devoted to peace than I am.

Map – President Lincoln tracked the Civil War's progress on a large map on his office wall. Colored pins stuck into the map indicated the positions of the various armies and navies.

N is for *Nancy*

Nancy Hanks Lincoln was Abraham's mother. Less than two years after the Lincoln family moved from Kentucky to Indiana she became deathly ill, and on October 5, 1818, she died. She was only thirty-four years old. Her husband, Thomas, made a coffin, and Abe whittled the pegs that held it together. In later years Abe paid his mother high tribute: "All that I am, or hope to be, I owe to my angel mother."

Nevada – Nevada was one of two new states to join the Union during Lincoln's administration. The other one was West Virginia.

Nickname – Abraham Lincoln had a number of nicknames. "Old Abe," "Honest Abe," "Rail Splitter," "the Backwoodsman," and "the Great Emancipator" were just a few.

Newspaper – Lincoln loved to read newspapers. At any given time he would subscribe to a dozen or more. Newspapers, said his law partner, were Lincoln's food.

I do not think much of a man who is not wiser today than he was yesterday.

When the hour comes for dealing with slavery, I trust I will be willing to do my duty though it cost my life.

O is for *Our American Cousin*

Lincoln was watching the comedy *Our American Cousin* at Ford's Theatre in Washington on the night of April 14, 1865. The third act had just gotten under way when an actor named John Wilkes Booth crept into Lincoln's box and fired a bullet into the back of the president's head. Lincoln was carried across the street to a boardinghouse, where he died the next day. The nation was plunged into mourning.

Oak Ridge Cemetery – Lincoln said, "When I die lay me in some quiet place." He got his wish: he, his wife, and three of their four sons are buried in Oak Ridge Cemetery in Springfield, Illinois.

Oyster – When Lincoln was reelected president in 1864, his supporters feasted on oysters. Lincoln dished them out himself.

Whenever I hear anyone arguing for slavery, I feel a strong impulse to see it tried on him personally.

QUIET PLEASE

P is for *Prank*

Lincoln's two youngest sons, Willie and Tad, were full of mischief. In Springfield they would come to their father's office and pull one naughty prank after another. According to Lincoln's law partner, William Herndon, the boys would throw books onto the floor, pour ink and ashes onto the books, "and then dance upon the pile." Lincoln never got angry—he thought they were good boys.

Pile – Lincoln was very disorganized when it came to his legal papers. In his office in Springfield he kept a pile of paper on the floor. On top of the pile could be found a handwritten note: "If you can't find it anywhere else, look here."

No man has a good enough memory to be a successful liar.

Tact: the ability to describe others as they see themselves.

Poetry – From time to time Lincoln liked to write poetry. This was especially true when he was young. One early poem ran: "Abraham Lincoln his hand and pen, / he will be good but god knows When."

Pacific Railway Act – In the 1850s Americans dreamed of having a railroad that ran from coast to coast. On July 1, 1862, President Lincoln signed the Pacific Railway Act, which helped make that dream a reality. Seven years later, in 1869, the eastern and western sections of the transcontinental railroad met in Promontory, Utah. America cheered.

It would do no good to go ahead any faster than the country would follow.

Postmaster – In 1833, when Lincoln was twenty-four, he was appointed postmaster of New Salem, Illinois. He liked the job because he could read all the newspapers for free before delivering them. Unfortunately he wasn't a very careful postmaster. Half the time he'd go off and leave the post office unlocked. People complained.

Q is for Quincy

In 1858, while running for the Senate, Lincoln had a series of public debates with Stephen A. Douglas. One of those debates took place in Quincy, Illinois, a town on the Mississippi River. Unlike Lincoln, Douglas wasn't bothered in the least by slavery, nor did he think it was something for the nation to go to war over. "Let each state mind its own business," he told the crowd in Quincy. "If we will stand by this principle, then Mr. Lincoln will find that this republic can exist forever divided into free and slave states." Lincoln strongly disagreed with Douglas's position, and often said so.

Quick – A photographer wanted to take a picture of Lincoln while he delivered the Gettysburg Address. But Lincoln's remarks were so quick that by the time the photographer got his camera set up, the speech was over. He missed the shot.

Quorum – Before any business could be conducted in the Illinois legislature, there had to be a quorum—that is, a minimum number of legislators present. Once, hoping to delay an important vote, Lincoln snuck out the window with two other like-minded politicians!

is for *Rider*

When he was a lawyer, Lincoln traveled by horseback throughout central Illinois, visiting courtrooms in the Eighth Judicial Circuit. Being a circuit rider was hard work. Roads were bad, and accommodations were scarce. Many lawyers hated riding the circuit. But Lincoln saw it as an excellent way to meet people and make himself more widely known.

Republicans are for both the man and dollar, but in case of conflict the man before the dollar.

Republican – In 1854 a new political organization was created, the Republican Party. Republicans opposed slavery, and Lincoln decided to join the new party. He was the second Republican to run for president and the first to be elected.

Robert – Born in 1843, Robert Lincoln was Abraham and Mary's eldest son. Unlike his playful younger brothers, he was a serious young man, and after his father's death in 1865 he tried to comfort and advise his grieving mother. In 1868 Robert married and started a family, and later he worked for the government and for a railroad company. He died in 1926.

S is for *Springfield*

In 1837 Abraham Lincoln moved to Springfield, Illinois, where he began to practice law. Two years later Springfield became the state capital. Still, in many ways it remained a small town. Hogs and cows wandered lazily up and down the streets. The hogs (or "porkers") were a real nuisance. They brought traffic to a stop and left a mess wherever they went. Abe had to look where he stepped as he made his way about town.

I do not lead, I only follow.

START

FINISH

Strike – When shoe factory workers went on strike in New England in 1860, Lincoln wholeheartedly supported their right to do so. "I like the system which lets a man quit when he wants to," he said. Thinking of the condition of slaves in the South, he remarked, "Thank God that we have a system of labor [in the North] where there can be a strike."

Sarah – Sarah Bush Lincoln was Abraham's stepmother. Unlike Abe's father, who discouraged his son from reading and writing, Sarah gave him all the encouragement she could. She also gave him plenty of love. "Abe was a good boy," she said. "His mind and mine . . . seemed to run together."

Simple – Lincoln tried to keep his speeches simple so people would have no trouble understanding them. But he knew he was bound to confuse some folks. As Lincoln liked to say, "There are always some fleas a dog can't reach."

Strong – Lincoln was surprisingly strong. One friend in Indiana recalled seeing him "carry a chicken house . . . that weighed at least six hundred pounds."

To sin by silence when they should protest makes cowards of men.

T is for *Tad*

Thomas Lincoln, or Tad as he was called, was Abraham and Mary's youngest son. He was a high-spirited child, always racing about, looking for fun. A secretary of Lincoln's said that Tad "gave to that sad and solemn White House . . . the only comic relief it knew." In her widowhood, Mary focused all her attention and love on young Tad, and she was devastated when he died of illness in 1871 at the age of eighteen.

Thomas – Abraham's father also was named Thomas. He was an uneducated man, and it irritated him that Abe's nose was always stuck in a book. The two had a tense relationship. "I never could tell whether Abe loved his father very well or not," a relative said. "I don't think he did." Thomas Lincoln died in 1851 and is buried alongside his wife Sarah in Shiloh Cemetery, in Coles County, Illinois.

Towering genius disdains a beaten path. It seeks regions hitherto unexplored.

Tall – Abe Lincoln was a tall man—six feet four inches, to be exact. Occasionally he would meet someone taller than he was. He said to a soldier who stood six foot seven, "Say, friend, does your head know when your feet get cold?"

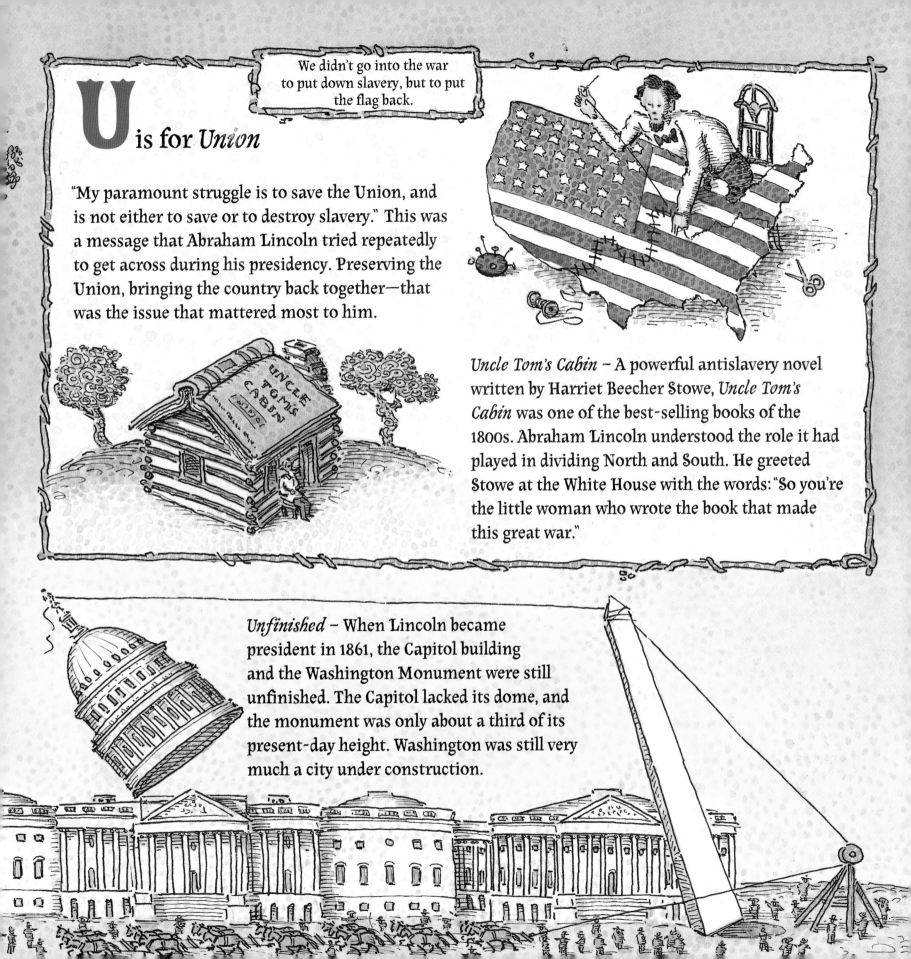

U is for *Union*

"My paramount struggle is to save the Union, and is not either to save or to destroy slavery." This was a message that Abraham Lincoln tried repeatedly to get across during his presidency. Preserving the Union, bringing the country back together—that was the issue that mattered most to him.

Uncle Tom's Cabin – A powerful antislavery novel written by Harriet Beecher Stowe, *Uncle Tom's Cabin* was one of the best-selling books of the 1800s. Abraham Lincoln understood the role it had played in dividing North and South. He greeted Stowe at the White House with the words: "So you're the little woman who wrote the book that made this great war."

Unfinished – When Lincoln became president in 1861, the Capitol building and the Washington Monument were still unfinished. The Capitol lacked its dome, and the monument was only about a third of its present-day height. Washington was still very much a city under construction.

V is for *Vote*

It pleased Lincoln to free the slaves by signing the Emancipation Proclamation, but as time went on he wanted to do more than that. Black men, he felt, should be able to vote, to have a say in their own government.

Sadly, Lincoln did not live to see his ambition realized. But four years after his death, in 1869, Congress passed the Fifteenth Amendment, granting all male citizens the right to vote regardless of "race, color, or previous condition of servitude."

VOTE

All should have   an equal chance.

BALLOT

The ballot is stronger than the bullet.

Vice President – Hannibal Hamlin, from Maine, was vice president during Lincoln's first term of office. Back then it was the political party, not the nominee, that selected the vice president. When Lincoln and Hamlin got together in Chicago after the election, neither could remember ever having met the other.

Andrew Johnson, from Tennessee, was vice president during Lincoln's second term of office. Upon Lincoln's death he became president, but he had no interest in helping black people as Lincoln had. In fact, he seemed determined to restore white supremacy to the South. Johnson made many enemies in Washington, and in 1868 he was nearly thrown out of office.

I am in favor of animal rights as well as human rights. This is the way of a whole human being.

W is for *Willie*

William Lincoln was the third of the Lincolns' four sons. He was a thoughtful, gentle, and pious child, adored by his parents. Like many boys at that time, Willie was fascinated by trains—how they were built and how they ran. He could recite the name of every train station between New York and Chicago.

When Willie died in 1862, at the age of eleven, his mother suffered a complete emotional breakdown. Lincoln told his wife that unless she learned to control her grief, he might have to send her to an insane asylum.

HOE! HOE!

Work – Abe wasn't lazy, exactly, but he didn't like to work any harder than he had to, especially when he was young. "I'd rather read, tell stories, crack jokes, talk, laugh—anything but work," he said.

Wrestler – Lincoln was a wrestler. A pretty good one, too.

Whiskers – When Lincoln was running for president, a girl named Grace Bedell wrote to him, encouraging him to grow whiskers: "You would look a great deal better for your face is so thin." Lincoln took her advice, and later, while passing through New York, he met Grace and was able to thank her in person.

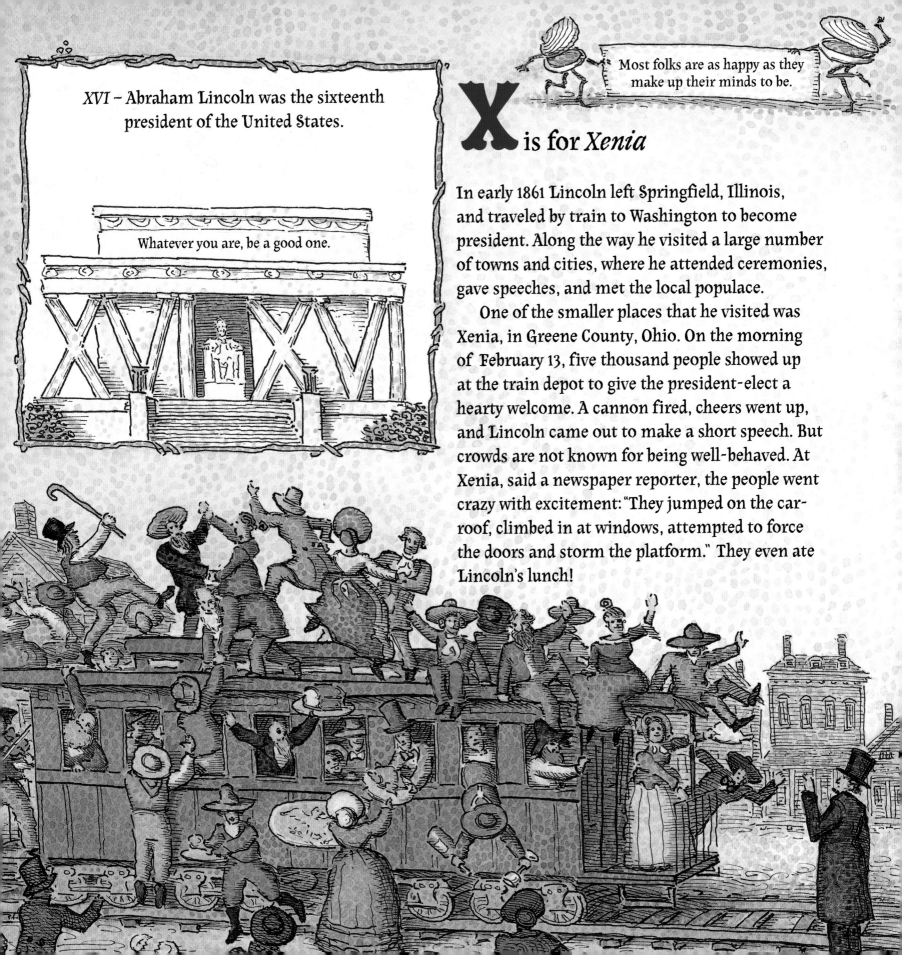

XVI – Abraham Lincoln was the sixteenth president of the United States.

Whatever you are, be a good one.

Most folks are as happy as they make up their minds to be.

X is for *Xenia*

In early 1861 Lincoln left Springfield, Illinois, and traveled by train to Washington to become president. Along the way he visited a large number of towns and cities, where he attended ceremonies, gave speeches, and met the local populace.

One of the smaller places that he visited was Xenia, in Greene County, Ohio. On the morning of February 13, five thousand people showed up at the train depot to give the president-elect a hearty welcome. A cannon fired, cheers went up, and Lincoln came out to make a short speech. But crowds are not known for being well-behaved. At Xenia, said a newspaper reporter, the people went crazy with excitement: "They jumped on the car-roof, climbed in at windows, attempted to force the doors and storm the platform." They even ate Lincoln's lunch!

Y is for *Yosemite*

When I do good, I feel good.
When I do bad, I feel bad.
That's my religion.

In 1864 President Lincoln signed an act that granted the Yosemite Valley and the nearby Mariposa Big Tree Grove to the state of California. The land was to be used, Lincoln said, for the public's enjoyment and recreation. Never before had the U.S. government set aside land for such a purpose. The Yosemite Valley Grant Act led, in time, to the National Park System.

EXP: 4.14.65

Yam – Lincoln's last meal, eaten on April 14, 1865, was simple and nourishing: soup, a roasted bird, and baked yams.

Yard Sale – Once, during the war, President Lincoln glanced out the window and saw his son Tad holding a yard sale. The boy was selling his parents' clothes to raise money to help support the Union troops. Lincoln put a quick end to that.

PRESIDENT'S DAY SALE

I can make more generals, but horses cost money.

Z is for *Zouaves*

Units of volunteer soldiers, the Zouaves were well known in the 1860s for their colorful uniforms and precision drill work. They could load, fire, and reload their weapons from any position, and do it in perfect unison. Lincoln enjoyed watching the Zouaves' drill routines, first in Springfield and later at the White House.

Zinc – Abraham Lincoln's profile appears on the penny. A humble man, Lincoln would be delighted to know that his image graces the humblest of all coins. Nowadays, despite their copper color, Lincoln pennies are made mostly of zinc.

And back to A . . .

In the end, it's not the years in your life that count. It's the life in your years.

ATOMIC NUMBER 30

Zn

65.39

A is for *American*

One principle, one dream, guided Lincoln during his four years in the White House: to preserve the Union, to join together North and South so that the country could once again move forward and be strong. Wise and generous hearted, Abraham Lincoln was a friend of human rights. He was a patriot, too. Nothing, he felt, was more important than the health and well-being of his country and its people.

Abraham Lincoln was proud to call himself an American.

For Penny Kastanis,
who makes good
things happen
A. S.

For Barbara and
Ed Omert
J. O'B.

I do the very best I know how—the very best I can;
and I mean to keep on doing so until the end.

Text copyright © 2015 by Alan Schroeder
Illustrations copyright © 2015 by John O'Brien
All Rights Reserved
HOLIDAY HOUSE is registered in the U.S. Patent and Trademark Office.
The illustrations were done in ink and condensed watercolors
on Strathmore Bristol paper.
Printed and Bound in October 2014 at Toppan Leefung, DongGuan City, China.
www.holidayhouse.com
First Edition
1 3 5 7 9 10 8 6 4 2

Library of Congress Cataloging-in-Publication Data
Schroeder, Alan.
Abe Lincoln : his wit and wisdom from A to Z / by Alan Schroeder ;
illustrated by John O'Brien.
pages cm
ISBN 978-0-8234-2420-7 (hardcover)
1. Lincoln, Abraham, 1809-1865—Juvenile literature. 2. Presidents—
United States—Biography—Juvenile literature. 3. Alphabet books—
Juvenile literature. I. O'Brien, John, illustrator. II. Title.
E457.905.S38 2015
973.7092—dc23
[B]
2013038989